www.FlowerpotPress.com
CHC-1010-0497
Made in China/Fabriqué en Chine

The FOREST MAN

The True Story of Jadav Payeng
by Anne Matheson and Kay Widdowson

Jadav Payeng loves trees.

He loves the sound of the wind rustling through their leaves.

He loves the feel of their bark—smooth on some trees, rough and bumpy on others.

He loves the birds in their branches and the animals that live in their shade.

As a young boy, Jadav and his family lived on the river island of Majuli in the middle of the mighty Brahmaputra River in India.

The island was a forest filled with a multitude of animals and surrounded by exotic birds in the sky and fish in the river.

Over time,
that all changed.

In this part of India, monsoons
blew in for weeks on end.
When this happened, the
Brahmaputra River crashed and
churned, washing water across the
island, leaving a path of destruction.

As the water retreated, the forests were washed away, leaving only sand. No trees where the birds could nest. No shade for the animals.

By the time Jadav reached the age of fourteen, the island was in danger of being slowly washed away.

Jadav believed his island could be saved.

On a barren sandbar on the coast of Majuli, he began to plant trees. With only a stick to dig a hole in the sand, Jadav planted twenty bamboo saplings.

He had only just begun.

Each day from that day forward, Jadav arose long before the sun came up to complete his chores and tend to his cattle.

Farm work finished, he would begin his long walk to the Brahmaputra River.

There, Jadav would climb into his
rowboat to cross the river and then
hop on his bicycle for the ride to his
forest, where he would plant and care
for his trees.

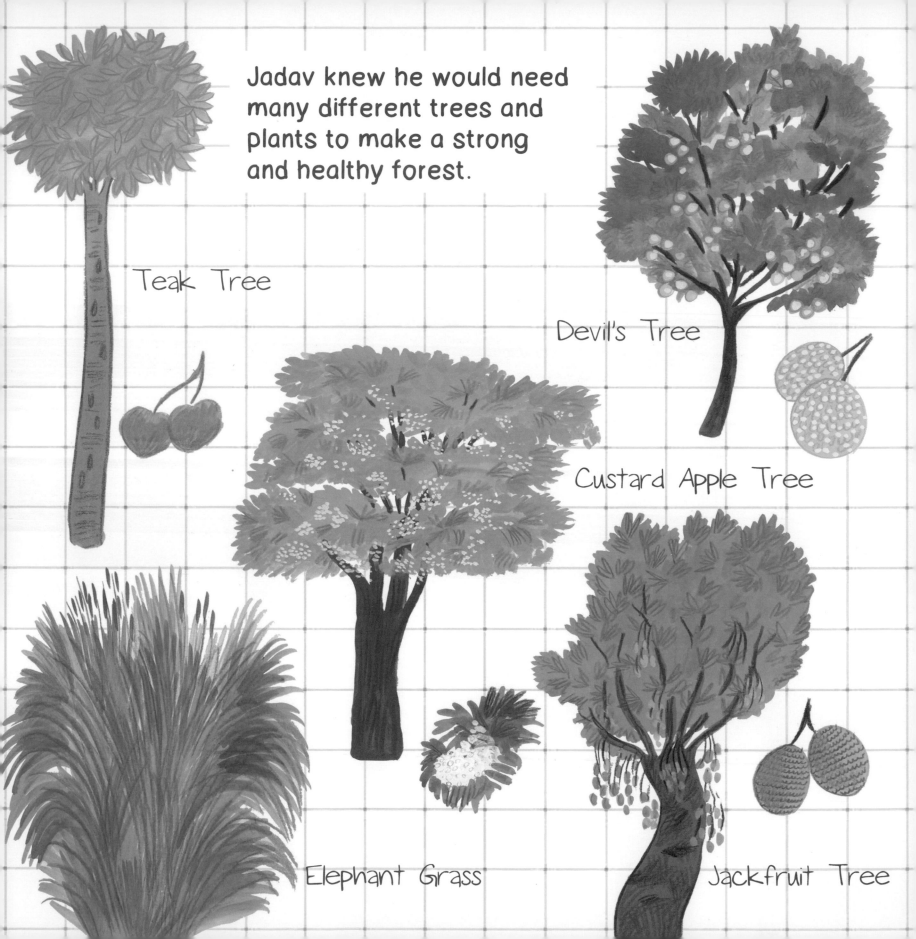

Jadav knew he would need many different trees and plants to make a strong and healthy forest.

Teak Tree

Devil's Tree

Custard Apple Tree

Elephant Grass

Jackfruit Tree

Banyan Tree

Star Fruit Tree

Mango Tree

Tamarind Tree

Jadav didn't just bring trees and plants to his forest. He also brought insects to help the trees pollinate and fertilizer from his cattle to help the trees take root. He was using nature to help rebuild his forest.

Day after day, year after year, Jadav continued to walk and then row and then ride and then plant.

Walk...

And then row...

And then ride...

And then plant...

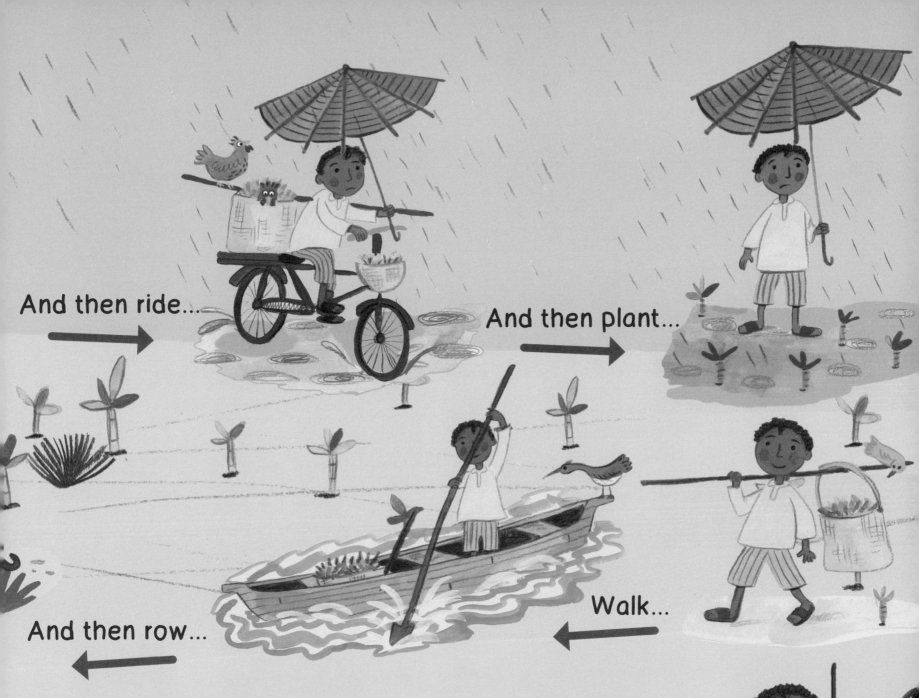

And then ride...

And then plant...

And then row...

Walk...

There were times the rain would thrash down for days on end, leaving Jadav fearing his forest would not survive.

Survive it did.

As Jadav kept planting his trees and tending his forest, incredible things happened.

The young saplings grew.
As they grew, they sprouted seeds.

The wind blew.
As the wind blew, it spread the seeds.

The seeds took root.
As the seeds took root, the trees grew.

The roots of the trees made the land stronger.
As the land became stronger, it held onto the
rainwater so the grass could grow.

Then the birds came back. The birds spread more seeds, the wind blew on, and the trees and the grass continued to grow.

Now that there was grass and leaves to eat, the animals returned. Cows and deer, monkeys and elephants, rabbits, tigers, and even a few rare one-horned rhinos.

Through all this growth, Jadav continued to plant his trees, as he does to this day.

And what has he accomplished?

Over forty years, one man, who loves his land, started with a handful of small trees and with the help of the wind, and the rain, and the insects, and the birds has built a beautiful forest.

Today, people from all over the world come to visit Jadav's forest. He welcomes the visitors and asks that they take the time to plant a tree, to remember his work when they return home, and to plant some trees there too.

Jadav's forest, Molai Forest, is not just an important place for Jadav, it has become a home for a number of endangered animals and animals who had lost their habitat to the extreme flooding and erosion. Within Jadav's sprawling forest, wild animals are now able to wander, graze, hunt, and gather. Can you find all of the animals from Jadav's forest throughout the book?

INDIAN RHINOCEROSES, also known as greater one-horned rhinoceroses, can live up to forty years in the wild!

CHITALS are also called spotted deer. These deer are native to India and are known for their white spots and the dark stripe down their back.

GANGES RIVER DOLPHINS are named after the other river they inhabit, the Ganges River. These dolphins are endangered as there are less than 2,000 of them left in the world.

WILD WATER BUFFALO are large herbivores native to India that spend most of their day submerged in bodies of water like the Brahmaputra River.

RED AVADAVATS are brightly colored red birds found across India. The bright red birds are usually male, while the females are typically a duller red color.

SLENDER-BILLED VULTURES were only recently recognized as their own species. They are one of the many types of vultures to return to Majuli after over forty years.

INDIAN ELEPHANTS have become regular inhabitants of Molai Forest. A herd of over 100 elephants have stomped through it and at least ten elephant calves have been born there.

BENGAL TIGERS are one of the biggest wild cats in the world. They are also the national animal of India.

Jadav's story is an important lesson in persistence and dedication. Jadav was able to create Molai Forest through reforestation. By planting trees in an area that was destroyed by flooding, Jadav was able to reclaim the land and help it thrive. His passion for growing his forest and planting trees has made a huge impact not only on the island of Majuli, but also on all those who have visited his forest, heard his story, and even been involved in reforestation themselves.

5

Monsoon season lasts about 5 months, from June to October, each year in India. Monsoons have been eroding the island of Majuli for decades, but through Jadav's efforts, plant life has been thriving and animals that had previously lost their homes are now able to come back to Majuli and live in Molai Forest.

2

It takes Jadav about 2 hours to get from his home to his forest. He has to travel by boat, bicycle, and foot both ways each day to care for his trees and protect the animals who call his forest home.

1979

Jadav began planting the trees which would eventually become Molai Forest in 1979, when he was about fourteen years old. He has since dedicated his life to developing his forest and helping it grow strong.

2015

In 2015, Jadav was honored with the Padma Shri, the fourth highest civilian award in India, for his efforts in replanting the land on Majuli. It is one of many awards and honors Jadav has received since his forest was publicized.

5,000

Jadav wants to plant 5,000 more acres, or about 2,023 hectares, of forest on Majuli in his lifetime. That is over three times what he has already planted! His dream is for his two sons to one day take over caring for the forest.

556

Jadav's forest is over 556 hectares, or 1,400 acres, in size. Imagine 1,000 football fields put together. That is roughly the size of Jadav's forest.

GLOSSARY

Accomplished – something that has been achieved or done successfully

Barren – land without plants or trees

Brahmaputra River – one of the major rivers that flows through Asia

Destruction – causing severe or extensive damage to something

Exotic – something that stands out because of bright coloring or because it is out of the ordinary

Fertilizer – a substance used to enrich the soil

Hectare – a measurement mainly used for land; one hectare is equal to about 2.5 acres

Majuli – the largest river island in the world, located in the middle of the

Brahmaputra River

Monsoon – a season that affects southwest Asia and nearby areas and is

characterized by very heavy rainfall

Multitude – a great number of people or things

Pollinate – transferring pollen from a male flower to a female flower

Reforestation – the process of replanting an area with trees and plants

Retreated – moved back or away from a position

Saplings – young trees with slender trunks

FURTHER READING

Dalal, A. Kamala. *India*. Countries of the World. Washington, D.C.: National Geographic Society, 2007.

Fontes, Justine, and Ron Fontes. *India*. AtoZ. Scholastic, 2003.

India. Eyewitness Books. New York, NY: DK Publishing, 2002.

Ryan, Patrick. **Welcome to India**. Mankato, MN: The Child's World, 2008.

Nardo, Don. *India*. Enchantment of the World. New York, NY: Scholastic, 2012.

Bartell, Jim. *India*. Exploring Countries. Minneapolis, MN: Bellwether Media, 2011.

To learn more about Jadav, go to
http://www.flowerpotpress.com/theforestman
for links to articles and videos.

In an effort to improve our world and in collaboration with Trees for the Future (TREES), a tree will be planted for every book purchased. Our plant a tree partnership is a way for us to assist TREES in their efforts to heal the environment and alleviate poverty for smallholder farmers in impoverished countries. To learn more about TREES, visit http://trees.org/.